freedom
to act

The "Harm Reduction for
Rural Youth" Project Experience

Supporting youth creating solutions for youth

Centre
for Addiction and
Mental Health
Centre de
toxicomanie et
de santé mentale

Addiction Research Foundation
Clarke Institute of Psychiatry
Donwood Institute
Queen Street Mental Health Centre

A World Health Organization Centre of Excellence

Freedom To Act
The "Harm Reduction for Rural Youth"
Project Experience

For more information on other Centre for
Addiction and Mental Health resource materials
or to place an order, please contact:
Marketing and Sales Services
Centre for Addiction and Mental Health
33 Russell Street
Toronto, Ontario M5S 2S1
Canada
Tel: 1-800-661-1111 or
(416) 595-6059 in Toronto
E-mail: marketing@camh.net

Visit our Web site at: www.camh.net

Disponible en français sous le titre
Liberté d'action : Projet de réduction des
méfaits chez les jeunes des milieux ruraux

FOREWORD

When HARRY Met Dunnville
Rural Teens Celebrate Launch

In the spring of 1999, with the annual high-school prom season on the horizon in Dunnville, Ontario, students at the local secondary school needed harm reduction strategies to avoid the dangers of drug or alcohol use.

Students gathered in the gymnasium for what they assumed would be the usual pre-prom exhortation against drinking and driving… They were wrong.

What the 750 students of Dunnville Secondary School saw was an example of what their own classmates — and by extension themselves — can do when they combine their skills and enthusiasm toward a common goal.

In front of the entire school population, and invited guests, three high school students presented the fruit of almost two years of work by themselves and others. The three were the creative team behind a student-created magazine, *Wild Times, Deadly Times,* which was subsequently given to every student in Dunnville Secondary School. The magazine was created to provide this small town's young people with information on how to avoid the perils associated with alcohol and drug use that often tragically claim the lives of rural youth.

At the heart of the project was the recognition that rural youth face problems distinctly associated with their environment, often different from the problems faced by their counterparts in large urban centres. Consequently, distinct methods of dealing with those problems in a small town setting needed to be developed.

The idea of a youth-driven harm reduction project came from a youth counsellor in Dunnville. The process was embraced wholeheartedly by the local community, which was obviously open to new ideas and had the foresight to care about the well-being of its future leaders.

The youth counsellor and the community joined forces with the Centre for Addiction and Mental Health (CAMH) to form the Harm Reduction for Rural Youth (HARRY) project team. The team resolved to take the lessons learned through a similar project *(Let 'Em Go*)* conducted in an urban community, and adapt them to fit the special needs of a rural community. The team members documented and evaluated every step taken in the project to ensure CAMH and others could learn everything possible from the experience. This guide shares the lessons learned from HARRY.

Who better than rural youth themselves to develop the ways and means of getting this much-needed information about alcohol and drug use out to the town's young people? Today's youth are endlessly creative, and given the chance and some measured guidance, are up to the task of solving their own problems. All they need is the "freedom to act."

*Let 'Em Go: The Street-Involved Youth Harm Reduction Project Experience, Centre for Addiction and Mental Health, 1998.

ACKNOWLEDGMENTS

WHO DEVELOPED THIS BOOK?

Freedom To Act was adapted by Angus Scott from
*Let 'Em Go: The Street-Involved Youth Harm Reduction
Project Experience* (Centre for Addiction and Mental
Health, 1998).

Additional help in developing this book was provided by:
Julia Greenbaum
Sharon LaBonté-Jaques
Cindy Smythe
Suzanne Witt-Foley

Comments on earlier drafts were received from:
Donna Beatty
Blanche Bénéteau
Andrea Stevens Lavigne
Michelle Ott

Copy edited by:
Honey Fisher

Publication designed by:
Mara Korkola

PARTNERS IN THE HARM REDUCTION FOR RURAL YOUTH PROJECT

*Addictions Division, Haldimand-Norfolk Regional Health
Department:*
Cindy Jennings
Mary Nemeth
Sharon Thomas
Peter Welch

Centre for Addiction and Mental Health:
Julia Greenbaum
Sharon LaBonte-Jaques (Project Leader)
Cindy Smythe
Suzanne Witt-Foley

Children's Aid Society of Haldimand-Norfolk

Dunnville Secondary School
(Grand Erie District School Board):
Joan Biliski
Roseann McCulley
Bob Ronald

Co-op Students:
Mike Feltham
Amber Flagg
Angie Kingsmill
Mike Reid
Jill Vaughn
Breanne Wildfong

LIST OF KEY POINTS AND HOW-TO SUGGESTIONS

TABLE OF CONTENTS

WHY THIS BOOK WAS WRITTEN

1

The purpose of this book is twofold. First, it tells the story of how a rural community was able to involve young people in an educational and action program. Second, and perhaps more important, it is a tool that you can use to work with youth in your own community to address issues and problems related to alcohol and other drug use.

The goal of the HARRY project was to inform young people about harm reduction in relation to the use of alcohol and other drugs. Youth members of the project team were actively involved in researching issues that were of concern to them and in developing a magazine to educate their peers.

What Is a Participatory Approach?

- involves both investigation and development
- does not involve outside "experts" studying people as if they were "subjects"
- gets people involved in researching, or educating others about their own issues
- deals effectively with issues that aren't addressed by more traditional methods
- is intended to improve the quality of life of the people involved
- recognizes that people's own knowledge and experience are legitimate tools in the search for solutions to their problems. After all, whose knowledge and experience could be more relevant?

What Participatory Investigation Methods May Include

- group discussions
- public meetings
- surveys
- fact-finding tours
- collecting resource material

What Participatory Education Methods May Include

- photo novellas
- popular theatre
- videos
- storytelling
- drawing
- magazines
- whatever works best for your group

Characteristics of Participatory Projects

- capture the participants' practical knowledge
- create an appreciation for, and build upon, the participants' real-life experience
- appeal to people who may be alienated by other kinds of research such as the written word or formal, scientific methods

Benefits of Involving Youth

When young people are involved in researching their own issues and developing their own solutions, those solutions work. Why?
Solutions developed by youth for youth are

- relevant to youth
- accessible to youth
- acceptable to youth
- able to reach youth.

The young people who participate in the project

- gain valuable experience
- gain useful skills
- feel empowered to make changes in their own lives
- feel equipped to make changes in their community.

The students could have developed a different product. Instead of a magazine, they could have chosen to develop a book or video. They might have organized a program or service. Regardless, this project gave them the tools to do what they thought was best, and moreover, to succeed.

This book illustrates the many benefits of involving youth in this kind of process. The two keys to the project's success are that it used a participatory approach and community partnerships.

The next step after investigation is development. The information learned from the research can be shared with the community through an educational product, program or service.

BACKGROUND TO
THE HARRY PROJECT

THE STARTING POINT

HARRY began when a youth counsellor working in Dunnville read about the Street-Involved Youth Harm Reduction Project (SIYHRP), a Toronto pilot program. SIYHRP inspired the youth counsellor to approach the Centre for Addiction and Mental Health (CAMH) with the idea of initiating a similar project in a rural setting. She felt Dunnville was a community open to new ideas with willing community partners available to make those ideas happen. Local CAMH staff saw the potential for this idea, developed a proposal for HARRY, and in 1997 launched the project.

Developing a Project Plan

- Assess needs within the community through research, observation and/or direct experience.
- Define needs accurately – consult with community experts, etc.
- Decide who will be involved in defining the needs, planning the project and participating at each stage.
- Develop a rough project plan.
- Include time lines – who will do what, when? What are your deadlines? Make sure you consider the needs of everyone involved.
- Include a budget taking into account the resources you will need during the planning stage right through to producing the product. How can you get funding? What can you get donated? How can you pool resources with others?
- Get feedback about the plan from community members and other experts.
- Use the feedback to finalize a realistic plan, including goals, participants, time lines and budgets.

"While analyzing the student survey we noticed that teens said that there is a lot of information in the community and it's easy to get, but it's not that useful. Maybe we could make something with information that would be useful for teens."

Youth team report

WHAT ISSUE DID HARRY ADDRESS?

We know that the use of alcohol and other drugs is common among young people. We also know that young people suffer harmful consequences from the use of these drugs. Despite our best efforts at prevention, use of alcohol and other drugs will probably continue. Recognizing this reality, it seems reasonable to turn a portion of our energies towards finding ways to reduce the harms suffered by our young people.

The two main goals of HARRY were (1) to provide harm reduction strategies to prevent and reduce perils related to substance use among rural youth, and (2) to increase our knowledge of effective methods of working in rural communities. Specifically, the project's objectives were:

- to identify community needs and acceptance of harm reduction
- to involve rural youth in the development of a harm reduction strategy
- to facilitate youth in developing a product within a time frame and budget that would meet the goals and needs identified by youth in the community
- to support youths' views and decisions
- to empower youth and increase their skills.

We divided the project into four phases. Phase One was the initial planning and proposal stage and laid the groundwork for the youth involvement that began in Phase Two. In Phase Two, the concept of harm reduction was researched, training was provided in needs assessment and report writing and a pilot needs assessment was conducted. The actual needs assessment was conducted in Phase Three and the information collected was used to generate a list of potential products. Phase Four saw the youth identify the product to be developed, create a magazine and launch it at the high school.

THE CONCEPT OF HARM REDUCTION

Harm reduction is a holistic way of looking at all of the factors affecting people's lives, and provides a context for understanding the risks they encounter. This might be related to drugs, as in the HARRY project, or to any other type of risk such as unsafe sex or bicycling without a helmet. Providing someone with a condom reduces the risk of that person contracting a sexually transmitted disease. The action is aimed at reducing harm, not at preventing people from having sex.

Harm reduction is a public-health approach. It aims to minimize the harms caused by certain conditions that pose serious risks to individuals, groups and society. Harm reduction is not about stopping people from doing something risky. It is about showing people how to more safely do whatever they choose to do.

Some people support the harm reduction approach because it respects the individual's right to make personal choices. Others like it because it's not judgmental or punitive. Still others feel it's more realistic than other approaches. The fact is that people will use alcohol and other drugs. Some will eventually change, reduce or stop their use when they feel ready to do so. The harm reduction approach strives to keep them out of hospital, jail or the morgue until they're ready to make that decision. It also focuses on changing public policy, laws and environmental conditions that make drug use even more harmful.

Harm Reduction

- provides factual information
- provides resources
- provides education
- teaches skills and strategies
- develops attitude changes
- works to change public policies
- is not focused on eliminating alcohol and other drug use
- minimizes the negative impact of drug use for the user, the community and society

What Harm Reduction and a Participatory Approach Have in Common

- Both are practical, user-oriented and non-judgmental.
- Both value people as experts in the harms in their own lives, given their practical knowledge and experience.
- Both build on the existing capacities, strengths and practices of the youth who participate.

"The law governs what is right and what is wrong for us so the youth go and carelessly and unsafely use drugs and drink, sometimes just to rebel. This causes them to use it wrongfully and add harm to themselves and others. If they were given choices, then they would probably use (substances) more carefully."

Youth team member

COMMUNITY
INVOLVEMENT

3

COMMUNITY PARTNERS

Partnerships and community involvement in the
HARRY project were the keys to its successful completion. Community partners who were on the project
team provided time, effort, energy, expertise and
tangible resources including office space, supplies, fax
machines and computers. Other community partners
who were not part of the project team also made
valuable contributions. New community partners joined
the project as additional needs and skills were identified. Later partners included the Children's Aid Society
of Haldimand-Norfolk, the administration at Dunnville
Secondary School, and the community's newspaper,
The Dunnville Chronicle. The team leader kept all
partners informed about the progress of the project,

relayed ideas back to the project team, and ensured everyone had a chance to contribute and become involved.

THE PROJECT TEAM

The project team consisted of youth from Dunnville Secondary School who were recruited through the co-operative education program, staff from the Addictions Division of the Haldimand-Norfolk Health Department and staff from CAMH. CAMH team members included staff from the different divisions of CAMH, including Community Health and Education; Social, Prevention and Health Policy Research; and Communications and Marketing.

Once we decided to produce a magazine, *The Dunnville Chronicle* provided technical expertise and advice on the actual writing and layout of the product. Youth team members worked at the newspaper's offices, and, using the computer and software facilities there, did the layout of the magazine under the supervision of the managing editor.

The Children's Aid Society (CAS) provided physical space within its building where the students worked each day, researching and developing the product. The CAS also provided other resources, including telephones, faxes, photocopying facilities and a receptionist.

Dunnville Secondary School's administration opened the co-operative education program — the source of our youth — to us. The school allowed the project team to conduct a student survey, to hold focus groups and to solicit suggestions regarding the content and title of the magazine. It also provided the event at which the product could be launched — an assembly involving the over 700 members of the student body.

"The actual learning experience was very good. But the moving around and changing of faces was hard to get used to."

Youth team member

What We Learned

- We discovered the need for ongoing open communication between the various members of the project. Roles and responsibilities of both the student participants and partners must be clarified and confirmed regularly.
- Flexibility is a quality we found extremely necessary. Staff changes among our partners, labour disruptions, office changes and school professional development days were just a few of the unanticipated disruptions that required us to be flexible and adaptable. These types of issues must be dealt with and taken into consideration when setting time frames for product development.
- Anticipate change, especially in long-term projects like this.
- A word about computers. While we gratefully received donations of computer equipment, we found the equipment was often out of date and unreliable. Up-to-date, reliable computer equipment is a necessity. One option to consider is leasing equipment rather than accepting hand-me-downs.
- Software programs unfamiliar to the students will cause delays.

YOUTH
INVOLVEMENT

4

YOUTH RECRUITMENT

Of course, the youths involved with the HARRY project were the most important members of the project team. They were recruited through the local high school's co-operative education program, a program that places students in work settings where they learn about real-life employment issues and also learn job skills. The students receive credits towards their high school education through participating in a co-op placement and are evaluated on their performance by both the workplace supervisor and the school. Each student who completed the 220-hour placement received two senior level secondary school credits. This resulted in a total of 1,980 hours being devoted to the HARRY project by our nine co-op students.

Youth participation can be secured through other sources, such as volunteer centres, recreation centres, religious organizations, youth groups, youth drop-in centres and newspaper advertisements.

Why We Chose Co-op Students

- They were members of our target group.
- Co-op students were more than volunteers; they had a responsibility to fulfil the co-op program requirements in order to receive their school credits.
- Co-op students were able to commit substantial time to the program on a daily basis.
- Co-op students had easy access to our target group through their high school, allowing them to conduct student surveys and use other information-gathering techniques.

YOUTH SUPERVISION

It is important for an adult team member to take the lead in working with youth. We used a supervisor because we were working within the structure of the school's co-op program. The supervisor worked in the same location as the youths and interacted with them on a daily basis. The supervisor and the youths worked together to set weekly work plans and goals and met on a regular basis to review progress. Other roles of the supervisor were to ensure that the necessary resources were available to the youths and to liaise with the co-op program and school administration as well as the rest of the project team.

We used a supervisor but there are various ways to structure the project so that one adult takes the lead in working with the youths. Other groups may wish to use a youth facilitator. The important point is to provide youth with support, guidance and encouragement. They need to feel connected to the project and to the other members of the team. The supervisor or facilitator is responsible for fostering this connection.

Qualities to Look for in a Youth Supervisor

- experience working directly with youth
- knowledge of the issues being addressed
- familiarity with the community of interest
- commitment to a participatory approach

An Effective Youth Supervisor

- empowers youth by giving them control over the way they conduct the research and develop the product
- allows youth to make their own decisions
- gives assistance, not orders
- shows confidence in the youths' abilities as individuals as well as team members
- provides support around personal struggles and practical issues

"It helped me work more independently without someone saying this is what you have to do, so do it. We did our own project with help from other people."

Youth team member

What We Learned

• It is important for the supervisor to maintain close contact with both the youth and the project team to ensure that all are kept up-to-date about the status of the project. Everyone needs to know what everyone else is doing.

• We found, when working with students, that they need direct, hands-on supervision on a daily basis. Without such supervision, tasks may not be completed and communication problems may multiply. Students often have limited work experience and need guidance.

• Students require good role modelling by adult team members, especially around issues such as exhibiting good work habits. Showing up for work on time, calling in when sick, respecting the importance of deadlines and being punctual and accountable are some of the behaviours that need to be emphasized.

• Support is a key element when working with youth. It is more than just looking over their shoulders; it's offering information and clarification and creating a supportive environment.

YOUTH SELECTION

HARRY was divided into four phases, the last three of which required youth involvement. Selecting the students best suited to work on the project depended on which phase we were in. Phase Two required library research skills, report-writing skills and the ability to work as a team member. Phase Three required computer skills, strong organizational skills and an interest in survey design. Phase Four required creativity, writing skills, and an interest in product development. Three students were available for each of these three phases and our selection of membership was based on trying to match as closely as possible abilities and interests with skills the required for that phase. We also looked for a general interest in drug and alcohol issues.

The co-op students were selected based on the following criteria. Each one

- was a senior student
- indicated an interest in social services, research, marketing, business and/or health
- showed an ability to work as a team member
- showed an ability to work independent of constant supervision
- demonstrated an ability to meet deadlines
- possessed non-judgmental, open-minded attitudes
- had connections with youth both inside and outside the school.

What We Learned

- Coping with teen interactions requires sensitivity and understanding.
- Ensuring the workload is equally shared by all members of the three-person team requires vigilance.
- The content of the product has to be accurate, yet you have to ensure that the youths feel that the product is their own. Make it clear from the outset that you will only make changes if content is inaccurate.
- If you become too critical, the youths become frustrated.
- Skills and qualities required of youth participants depend on the nature of the youth project.

A suggestion for future initiatives would be to take advantage of the benefits provided by e-mail communication. This would allow for draft versions of the product to be sent for review, which would result in a quicker turnaround time, and students could check in via e-mail upon arrival each day.

YOUTH EMPOWERMENT

The HARRY project was committed to a participatory approach. The students were interviewed after the project to determine if this commitment was kept. It was important for us to know whether they felt that their ideas were heard and that they had made meaningful contributions to the project. The youths told us they felt they had had a great deal of input into what was produced and the overall look of the product. All of them also stressed that while it was a group effort, they believed their individual contributions were also reflected in the magazine.

Another indicator of empowerment was the skills gained during the project. Youth team members identified the following as skills and values they learned as a result of their participation:
• magazine production, editing, page layout
• research (conducting surveys and interviews)
• decision making by consensus
• group work and communication
• time management
• working with bureaucracies/government agencies.

Values included:
• harm reduction
• confidentiality
• responsibility
• open-mindedness.

Types of Youth Involvement
• becoming a team member
• participating in research as survey respondents
• participating in focus testing of the draft product
• using the final version of the product
• contributing material to the product
• suggesting titles for the product

How to Create an Empowering Environment for Youth
• Respect the youths and their input.
• Create a safe and affirming environment.
• Offer a fun, enjoyable experience.
• Establish trust and rapport.
• Demonstrate that the entire team is not just listening to the youths but is also following their advice.
• Give them the power to make decisions and let them put that power to use.
• Reward them.

"Dunnville is a small community and the youth of today will be the future adults. They will be the ones supporting this community. So if Dunnville's youth live in a town where the worries of harm in drug use, alcohol use and the worries of harm in our every day lives are reduced, then it will make this town a much better place to live for everyone in the community."

Youth team member

"I liked learning how a magazine is created and knowing that something I did could help someone in the future."

Youth team member

"The project has been a very good learning experience. The time spent doing all the work we have done makes me feel good inside. …I'm proud to know that we are helping to make a difference in our community."

Youth team member

ORIENTATION

We tried to anticipate which skills the students would need to accomplish each phase of the project, and build our training program around those needs. Skill areas covered included library research, internet use, data collection, analysis, and storage, and product development. Relevant in-service training was scheduled throughout the project and was provided by adult team members as well as community partners as required. It was important that youths understand the difference between the concepts of prevention and harm reduction. Some of the exercises performed during the orientation demonstrated these differences.

We did a team building exercise at the start of each phase as our membership tended to change at those stages. It was important for all to feel invested in the upcoming plans and feel a part of the team. Our hand-written contract exercise offered the opportunity for all to indicate what qualities of teamwork they valued and what qualities they felt were detrimental to the team concept. We performed the exercise by tracing out hands on paper and writing positive, valued qualities on the fingers and palms. The negative and detrimental qualities were written outside the hand, as they worked against team cohesion. We then cut out our ideas and glued them all onto a piece of bristol board. These positive and negative qualities served as a constant reminder of our ideas about teamwork and could be referred to when discussing issues related to team performance.

GATHERING
INFORMATION

5

DATA COLLECTION

The youths' task was to create a product based on the information they collected that would educate other youth about harm reduction. In order to accomplish that task, they had to learn data collection skills, including what questions to ask, how to ask them and whom to ask. When designing questionnaires, students developed questions that they felt were important. This spoke to one of the fundamental issues of HARRY — whose project is this? In the end, students may have asked some less relevant questions and actually missed some critical questions that may have added clarity. For example, they neglected to ask what specific harms rural youth might be experiencing.

What Does a Data Collection Phase Involve?

- defining exactly what issue you want to study
- defining specifically what you want to know about it
- deciding upon the best way of getting information (choosing a method – Interviews? Focus groups? Questionnaires? Reviewing existing materials? Covert observations?)
- determining whom you need to talk to and how to get them to participate (how will participating benefit them?)
- making sure every question you ask is designed to get the information you need (you may end up rejecting really interesting questions because they are not on topic).
- if the goal refers to harm reduction, asking questions about harm reduction
- considering ethical issues about probing into people's private lives
- planning how you will analyze the information you collect
- starting to think about the product you will develop to share your findings
- thinking about how information will be used

Survey Tip

Suggest to students that, when they design a survey, they think carefully about what they need to know versus what would be interesting or fun to know. Also suggest they think about what they are going to do with the information once they have it. People sometimes get caught up in the pursuit of what they think is interesting without considering its usefulness.

"The one question which we got a lot of responses to was the question about what types of drugs do teens want to know more about. The drug most teens want to know about is marijuana."

Youth team report

An attempt was made to get a representative sample of students to respond to the questionnaires. Samples were drawn from both sexes in each grade level, and, we hoped, from each category on the drug-use continuum, from abstainers to heavy users. We intended to sample 20 per cent of the student body of the school, but 50 per cent were actually sampled. This was due to overcalculating the size of the school's student body.

Also sampled were adults who are in close contact with youth and the community. Among those adults were teachers, police, parents, politicians, people who work in social service agencies, nurses and youth leaders. The intent of the adult questionnaires was to determine what adults thought were the harms being experienced by local youths, to assess their awareness of the harm reduction approach, and to determine the level of acceptance for such an approach.

If we had discovered that a majority of adults opposed the harm reduction approach, it would have been difficult to gain public acceptance of this product. Interestingly, adults appeared more accepting of the harm reduction approach and principles than did the students.

FOSTERING PUBLIC ACCEPTANCE OF HARM REDUCTION CONCEPT

We used several strategies to gain the public's acceptance of harm reduction. We used the survey to interview leaders within the community and we provided information for local newspaper articles at various stages of the project. We also made presentations to local service clubs, set up displays at the secondary school, and made presentations to councillors of the Regional Municipality of Haldimand-Norfolk.

We welcomed input throughout the project. We made a decision to go back to the high school students themselves for the title of the magazine and other sections such as an "Ask Us" page that answered common student questions.

The principal of the high school was asked to sign off on all materials produced for the magazine. This was a precautionary measure to prevent thousands of magazines sitting in boxes because the principal refused to allow their distribution.

All of these strategies helped foster acceptance of the magazine and the harm reduction concept.

Why did we take such a cautious, inclusive approach? Harm reduction is a fairly innovative approach and can be controversial. Public acceptance was important to maintain credibility and good working relationships within the community. The approach would help pave the way for support of other related work within the community, such as OPHEA's Alcohol, Cannabis and Tobacco Health Promotion Project for Youth (ACTION).*

What We Learned
• In Dunnville, community leaders we surveyed seemed more accepting of harm reduction than youth, which was both surprising and encouraging. This indicates a real shift in people's attitudes.

WHY WAS THE SURVEY METHOD SELECTED?

Phase One of the HARRY project did not involve students. This phase was used to secure partnerships and resources, as well as to develop project plans and information packages for student interviews. Phase Two of the project investigated different methods of collecting information.

The students received training in needs assessment and in techniques for collecting information. Pilot testing was done by the students using two methods — focus groups and surveys. The youths decided to hold two focus groups with male and female students from grades 9 through 12. However, after this experience,

What Is a Focus Group?

A focus group:

• is a structured group interview
• brings together a group of people to talk about a specific topic
• has six to 10 participants
• takes up to two hours.

Note: Do not include too many people in the focus group or it can become unruly and some people will not have a chance to speak. Too few people is not ideal either because people feel shy and the creative flow of sparking ideas off each other may not happen. A short time span is too rushed whereas an overly long one is too boring.

* © *Ontario Physical and Health Education Association (OPHEA), 1996*

they decided they weren't comfortable with the focus-group method. Given the time constraints of the project and logistics of the rural situation, it was difficult for us to provide the youths with the further training needed to increase that comfort level.

The pilot testing of the survey method proved more successful. After piloting the survey in several classes, the youths felt more comfortable with this method of data collection.

We consciously decided not to include samples of our surveys in this book because we don't want to influence other communities' survey design. Other communities can develop surveys specific to their project needs and should consider encouraging their youth to take ownership of whatever is developed.

What We Learned

- Pilot testing was important because we learned which method of data collection would better suit our project. We also came to understand the importance of balancing youth ownership of the project with achieving the goals of the survey.
- We discovered the need to verify numbers. For example, we relied on an inaccurate number when choosing our sample of the secondary school population.
- Students learned the value of pilot testing and the length of time it takes to conduct a survey. Through pilot testing they learned it took an average of two minutes to do a survey rather than the 20 minutes they had estimated.
- The pilot test allowed the youths to refine the contents of the survey.

Why a Needs Assessment Is Important

Too often, experts tell individuals and communities what they need and what they want. However, it is valuable to do some preliminary research with the people who will actually use the product or program to find out what they themselves believe they need and want. After all, they are the experts on their own lives and communities. They have perspectives and insights that can only come from first-hand experience.

DATA ENTRY AND ANALYSIS

If you are going to collect data, you need a method of coding and analyzing it. You must ask yourself ahead of time whether you can do it by hand or whether you have the computer software and expertise to manage the data.

You also need to consider how you are going to organize and handle questionnaires, and you must give particular thought to confidentiality issues. We coded our results by class, but there are other ways of doing it. Expertise in this area is needed to be successful. You have to ask yourself if your team has that expertise. If not, can you find it among your community partners or do you have the budget flexibility to hire outside help?

What We Learned
- A lot of thought has to be put into data entry and analysis ahead of time or you could run into problems.
- You need to ensure ahead of time that you have reliable computer hardware and data management software.

SYNTHESIZING AND INTERPRETING FINDINGS

After the youths entered the survey information into a data software program, they were ready to analyze the data. Two kinds of data were collected. The first kind was quantitative data, which included responses to questions designed to determine the percentage of people who thought alcohol use was a problem in the community. The second kind of data was qualitative — responses to open-ended questions such as ideas around harm reduction strategies. If you don't have access to people who can do survey analysis, you will probably want to collect your information in a

different way, such as through focus groups. Although analyzing focus group data can be time consuming, you could do the analysis yourself if you use small samples and fewer questions.

The team examined these results to look for useful ideas for their future product. Their analysis showed that over 80 per cent of the youths surveyed believe there is a drug problem in their community with the major consequences being school absenteeism and suspensions. Most of the youth blamed boredom — a lack of things to do —and suggested ways of alleviating this problem. Surveyed teens also indicated preferences for the medium through which they would receive information about alcohol and drugs and harm reduction strategies: 83 per cent said a video would be the best way to deliver information, with a magazine following as a close second. A majority said the best place to obtain this information would be at school.

Among the adults surveyed, a large majority felt drug and alcohol use was a big problem within the community. At the same time, about 79 per cent of adults surveyed felt harm reduction strategies such as designated driver programs were a good idea.

DEVELOPING
THE PRODUCT

CHOICE OF PRODUCT

We began Phase Four with a discussion about what product we would develop. Close attention was paid to suggestions made on the surveys. The group ranked the list of possible products in terms of three criteria:
• effectiveness
• "do-ability"
• how much the members would enjoy working on the product.

We selected the product with the following goals in mind. To
• educate rural youth about safer use of alcohol and other drugs
• be appropriate for our target group
• be accessible to our target group

- be a well-crafted product that the youths could be proud of
- present accurate and meaningful information
- be entertaining and light-hearted where appropriate
- be based on the information gathered through our research
- be acceptable to the community.

With these goals in mind, the students made the choice to produce a magazine. The magazine format was popular because it was accessible and user friendly. It could be read privately and could reach a large number of people. It could also be kept and re-read at the leisure of the target group. Furthermore it was a financially feasible format.

Before the final decision was made, we took into consideration distribution and ensured that the secondary school administration would agree to help with this.

What We Learned
- We learned the importance of letting the youths make the final decision on the product. There were other possibilities that could have been pursued such as restaurant-style table-top displays and bush party brochures. While we originally liked these ideas, they were not acceptable or of interest to the students themselves.

PRODUCT DEVELOPMENT

Having made the decision as to which product to create, the team felt inspired and filled with renewed purpose. We were energized and eager to get on with the task ahead. We were, however, a little concerned about what we had taken on. What kind of technical skills and resources would a magazine require?

What Does a Development Phase Involve?
- being realistic about the resources you have available, including equipment, materials, interest and talent
- defining clearly what you discovered through your research
- using the findings from your research to define clearly what kind of product will be most useful for your target audience and what can be realistically accomplished — a program? a service? a poster? an educational book, magazine, video, or play?
- looking at samples of similar products and learning from others' successes and mistakes
- finding ways to be participatory — involve the intended audience in the product development
- determining how best to distribute and advertise your product
- reviewing the developing product on an ongoing basis to ensure accuracy

Although we would have loved to acquire expertise in the print media field, we knew the team could not master those skills within the tight time frame allotted to us. We knew we would need resources outside the project team and found them at *The Dunnville Chronicle.*

One important concern was ensuring the acceptance of the magazine by the partners, the school and the community. Therefore, we took the precautions outlined earlier in this book, of having the high school principal and CAMH sign off on each page before it was released. By doing this, we assured the accuracy of the materials contained within the magazine, and maintained the school principal's support for the project.

MAKING THE MAGAZINE

Once again it was time to draw on the many skills of the project team. A team member with experience in the print media field helped us determine what physical resources we would need. This involved thinking about binding, printing requirements, costs, paper types, and the options regarding use of black and white, spot colour and process colour.

The youths decided the content of the magazine and also delegated the writing and other tasks that needed to be done. A page release schedule detailing the dates to complete material for pages and the dates these pages were to be completed, was drawn up with the community newspaper.

The youths drew on their own experiences, the research of previous youth team members and CAMH for the written and visual content of the magazine.

"The most beneficial aspect of the placement was working at The Chronicle *and working on the magazine by ourselves."*

Youth team member

"I liked learning how a magazine is created and knowing that something I did could help someone in the future."

Youth team member

As each article or picture was finished, it was submitted to the community newspaper where it was input into its computers. On a weekly basis, the students spent a half day at the newspaper office and, following the previously created page-release schedule, were given direction on page layout. Under the guidance of experienced staff, the students did the layout of the pages themselves. Drafts of these pages were then sent off to be reviewed for content accuracy by CAMH staff and for sign-off approval by the principal. Suggested changes were made each week during visits to the newspaper office.

During this phase of the project, students solicited input from their classmates and came up with *Wild Times, Deadly Times* as the title for the magazine.

LAUNCHING
THE MAGAZINE

The launch of the magazine, *Wild Times, Deadly Times,* was organized in conjunction with the local secondary school. Enough magazines were printed to allow distribution to every student within the school with extra copies available for the incoming class of the next school year.

We discussed several ways of distributing the magazine. We didn't like the idea of students receiving the magazine in class, because without any explanation of what it was, they might not have been interested in looking at it and might have just tossed it away.

A better bet, we decided, was to hold an assembly centred around the harm reduction theme. It was held a week prior to the annual high school prom and was a perfect fit. The assembly included a comic, yet informative, presentation about harm reduction.

The information was presented in a fun, youth-oriented way that piqued the interest of the students. During this assembly, the HARRY project team and magazine were presented to the student body. The students were then informed the magazine would be distributed in their homerooms the following morning. They were told that if they didn't want to keep the magazines, they could hand them in so other students would have a chance to read and use them.

The school was extremely co-operative about this distribution process and even gave homeroom teachers extra time to discuss the magazine.

"A lot of times people are afraid to ask people they know for help if they have a problem. This magazine is useful because you can look it up yourself instead of having to go ask someone."

Dunnville teen, following magazine launch

"I knew they were working on it, but I thought it was just a pamphlet or something. It's got a professional quality to it that I didn't expect."

Dunnville teen, following magazine launch

"It's got some good information in it, a lot of it I don't think people know."

Dunnville teen, following magazine launch

LEARNING FROM THE PARTICIPATORY EXPERIENCE

There were many issues to consider when developing time lines for the HARRY project. We always had to be mindful of the fact that we were dealing with students. Work plans had to be developed and clearly spelled out as did the time lines and tasks. Monthly calendars were useful in assisting students to plan ahead. Unexpected events and challenges such as computer problems, staff changes and labour disruptions, professional development days, fiscal year ends and co-operative education program calendars all had to be considered when setting realistic time lines.

For the young people, creating the magazine was the most fun and worthwhile part of the project. They were confident they had the skill and talent to do it; they needed only the resources and technical support.

The youths had a big investment in the project; their work would be seen by everyone within the school and they wanted it to be as professional and useful to those fellow teens as possible.

USING CO-OP STUDENTS

The school's co-operative education program was instrumental in ensuring youth participation in the project. The relationship that developed between the HARRY team and the school co-operative education program turned out to be beneficial to HARRY, the students who participated and the school itself.

The co-op program did pose special problems, however. As this project was two years in duration, and spanned three school terms, it was not possible to retain the same youth team for the length of the project. With each new term, we had to recruit, interview and select a new trio of students. This meant we had to repeat orientation procedures at the start of each of the three terms. As it turned out, there was always an overlap between student groups. At least one student from the first group was on board with the second group, and one student from the second group remained on board for the third. Thus, we always had someone with experience from the previous phase. That was unplanned and unanticipated, but did work in our favour. It provided a measure of continuity throughout the project.

COMMITMENT

The youths all admitted that, while they had some interest in drug-use issues, they took the co-op initially because it provided them with credits towards their Ontario Secondary School Graduation Diploma as well as valuable work experience. As time and the project proceeded, the project became more important to them personally and they took on greater ownership of the

"The time we have spent doing all the work we have done makes me feel good inside and I am also proud to know we are helping to make a difference in our community."

Youth team member

goals of the program. While this did not occur with all students, it was particularly noticeable with the final trio who produced the magazine. The team's job was to create an environment where the youths could freely and successfully do the work they had been recruited to undertake.

Reliance on the co-op program did create some unforeseen problems. The project lost two of the initial six students. They either lost interest in the project or quit school because of other pressures.

What We Learned
- It is important to have a match between the student and the placement.
- We had to consider the impact on the project if a youth dropped out of school or the program.
- We learned to respect the decisions made by some youths to drop out of the project and to move on.
- Outside influences on the students had to be kept in mind.

MAINTAINING TEAM COMMITMENT

The members of the team had a strong commitment to the participatory approach, especially one that was youth driven. We knew we would end up with a more user-friendly product by having the young people themselves actually create it. Due to the geographic realities of the area, we held fewer meetings in the early stages in an attempt to save money. However, we were forced to increase the frequency of meetings because we became concerned that the team members didn't have enough of a sense of involvement and the youths needed more supervision.

"The project taught me many things I never knew and it was the best work experience I have ever had."

Youth team member

Maintaining Commitment

The issue of completion is very important when working with youth. Many young people often feel impatient and easily discouraged. They may lack experience in finishing projects or resolving conflict. They may have encountered more failure than success. The project team has to decide how much to invest in a young person's staying with the project. The team members must be careful not to be excessive in their encouragement to the point of becoming disrespectful of the person's right to leave. They also need to be aware when support becomes too much like therapy.

What We Learned

- Make sure the team members' roles are clear.
- Make sure the team members' tasks are clear.
- Be clear about what their roles and tasks do not entail.
- Be aware of team members' expectations and hopes.
- Give members room to participate. They should not just be "talking heads." Participation must be relevant to be meaningful.
- Allow members to see the project they are working on first-hand. Avoid keeping them at arm's length.
- Build in ways to maintain their interest over the whole project by giving them meaningful work to do.
- Recognize that different members have different skills to be used at various stages of the project.
- Be aware that committees evolve and roles will change and develop.
- Keep in touch between meetings to ensure perceptions and feelings are clear.
- Ensure there is consensus about roles, tasks and project goals.
- Learn to place trust in the youth and respect their decisions.

PROJECT EVALUATION

CAMH held focus groups within the high school following the launch to assess student reaction to the magazine. Focus groups involved students from grades 9 through 12. The results from the focus groups were positive. Students from Grade 9 up to Grade 12, for the most part, understood the harm reduction message contained within the magazine. Among students in different grades, we found differing opinions about the magazine. It was difficult to create a product everyone liked. We found the younger students felt they gained more new information, while the older students wanted more credit given to the youth members of the project team, even though those youths had decided they did not want to take individual credit.

Youth Empowerment Achieved

One of the HARRY project's initial goals was to empower local youths by making them cognizant of their own talents and strengths and abilities to solve their own problems. An indication that HARRY succeeded in this purpose is illustrated in the following two examples:

- One student, previously shy and reserved, was so empowered through her association with the project that she was able to present at a conference of adult delegates on her involvement and feelings about HARRY.
- At the magazine launch, all three students had gained the confidence that enabled them to speak in front of hundreds of students and teachers about their involvement with the HARRY project.

CONCLUSIONS

9

The Harm Reduction for Rural Youth project was successful on many levels. The young people who participated found it a rewarding endeavour. They were proud of the work they had done and the magazine they had created. They learned new skills and gained self-awareness and self-confidence. The project team learned valuable lessons about how to be successful when pursuing participatory projects.

The youths and adults who were involved in the project felt positively about the experience. They enjoyed working with each other and were proud to have been a part of HARRY. The success of this project was also evident in the community partnerships forged. At the same time, the project wasn't expensive, because in-kind contributions from partners made it financially feasible. There was also a positive end product — a magazine distributing harm reduction information to Dunnville's youth. They were able to read a professional-looking magazine, written and created by their peers, which provided useful information in a format they could relate to easily. The intent is that information in the magazine will influence their approach to alcohol and other drugs in the coming years.

WHAT WAS SUCCESSFUL ABOUT THIS PROJECT?

It achieved its short-term objectives:
- The project was participatory, involving rural youth, community members, schools and CAMH staff.
- It identified community needs and fostered acceptance of harm reduction.
- It developed and created a product within a time line and budget.
- The product was developed by and for rural youths.
- The project was youth driven — they had control over what they produced.
- HARRY supported the youths' views and decisions.
- The youths felt empowered and increased their skills.

FUTURE INDICATORS OF SUCCESS

"If this project works for Dunnville and reduces alcohol and drug use… in this small community, then maybe it will influence other small communities to use these harm reduction strategies…"

Youth team member

In the long term, we hope that:
- The magazine will continue to be read by youth.
- Fewer people may be harmed in unsafe situations by practising harm reduction strategies.
- Youth agencies and the schools in Dunnville will use the magazine to increase awareness about harm reduction strategies.
- The work will attract public attention and break new ground.
- Other communities will do similar projects by learning from this process.

"I enjoyed the people I worked with and the goal we were working towards. I enjoyed working within a group and I believe it was very successful."

Youth team member

"I think (we) did a good job working as a team and getting the magazine done."

Youth team member

It's our hope that others who study this project will feel inspired to reach out within their own communities and help young people to not only increase their own skills, but to take ownership of, and improve, issues within their community. The imagination and skills displayed by the young people who participated in HARRY inspired the adults and other youth around them. It proves that adults must give youth the "freedom to act."

CPSIA information can be obtained at www.ICGtesting.com
Printed in the USA
241379LV00004B/66/P